Little Histories
for Little People

PAGE PUBLISHING, INC.
Conneaut Lake, PA

First originally published by Page Publishing 2021

ISBN 978-1-6624-1748-1 (pbk)
ISBN 978-1-6624-1749-8 (digital)

Printed in the United States of America

Little Histories for Little People

Abraham Lincoln

SARAH STILLMAN

Born into life when times were tough, Abe studied and saved till he had enough.

He briefly went to school but never got a degree.

Still, a lawyer for the people he would be.

He became president in 1861.
He wanted a brighter future for the country and his sons.

The north and the south soon began to fight.

So Abe prayed to God and asked what was right.

He sided with the north, or the union, they were called.

They wanted to end slavery and have freedom for all.

GETTYSBURG

The north was losing until they fought at Gettysburg one day.

GETTYSBURG

Abe gave his great speech, a speech still heard today.

A few years passed, and the union finally won.

Abraham Lincoln declared freedom, freedom for everyone!

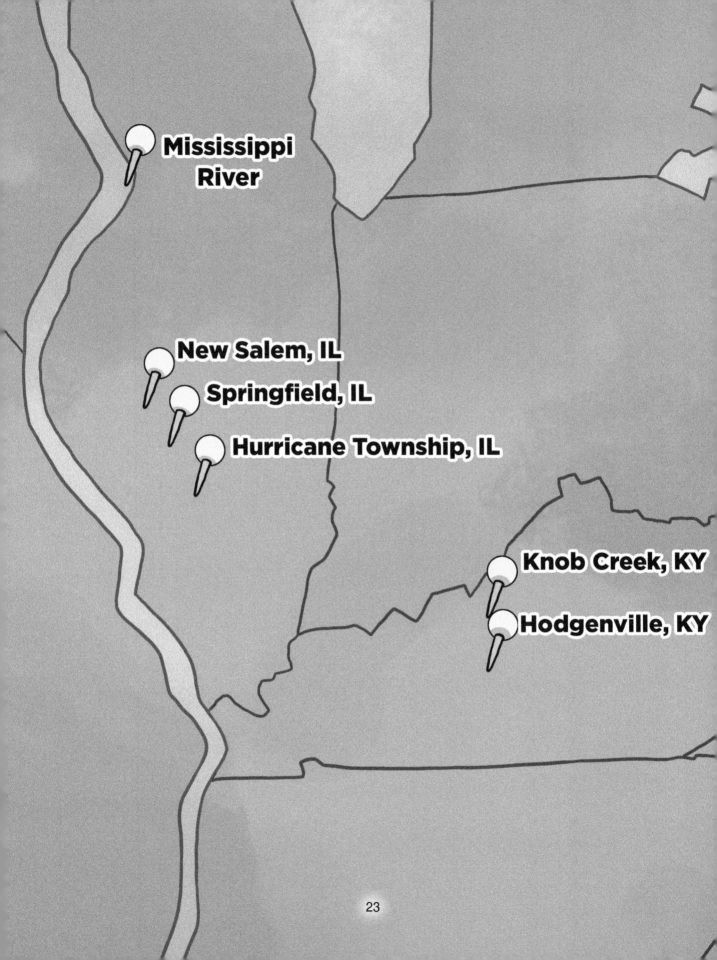

Mississippi River

New Salem, IL

Springfield, IL

Hurricane Township, IL

Knob Creek, KY

Hodgenville, KY

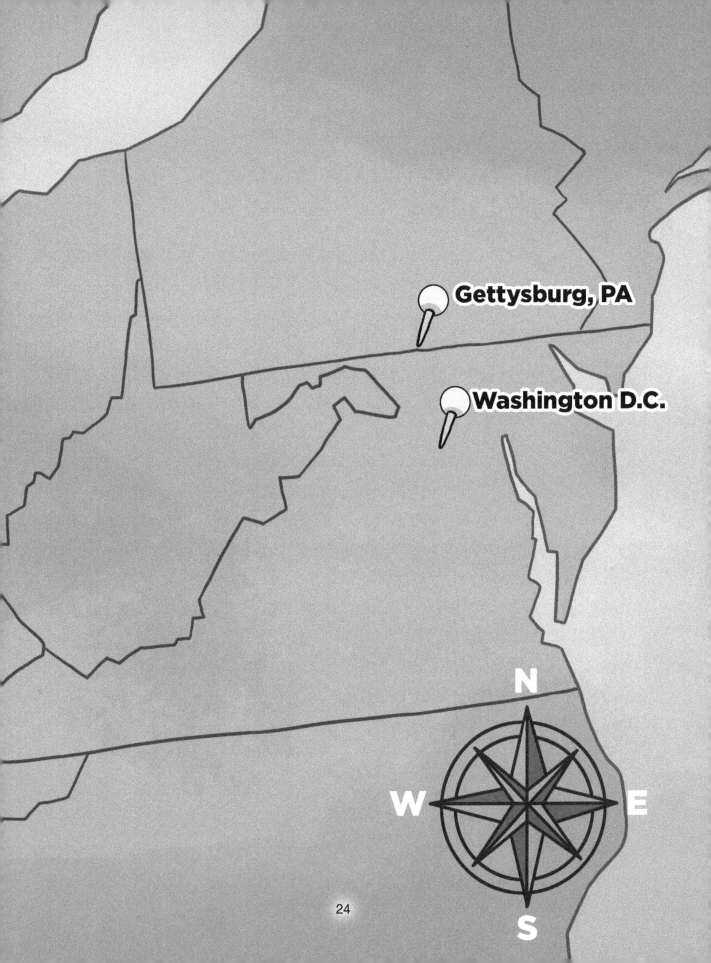

Gettysburg, PA

Washington D.C.

N

W

E

S

About the Author

 Sarah currently resides in Tavares, Florida, with her husband and two children. She graduated from the University of Florida with a degree in Geography and currently works as a LiDAR mapping scientist in the geospatial sector. She's always been fascinated by maps and different places around the globe, so she found a career that allowed her to follow her passion.

In her free time, she enjoys traveling with her family and friends and spending time out on the water. Sarah's love for history comes from her father, who has always encouraged her to pursue some form of writing. At home, Sarah and her husband enjoy watching shows and reading books based on historical events. Writing Children's history books has allowed Sarah to pass on that interest to her children in a fun and relatable way!

CPSIA information can be obtained
at www.ICGtesting.com
Printed in the USA
BVHW021835070421
604432BV00016B/648